First published in Great Britain in 2005
by **Artnik**
341b Queenstown Road
London SW8 4LH
UK

ISBN 1–903906–94–6

Design: Supriya Sahai
Pictures: Live Photography
Book Concept: Nicholas Artsrunik
Editor: John McVicar

Printed and bound in Spain by Gráficas Díaz

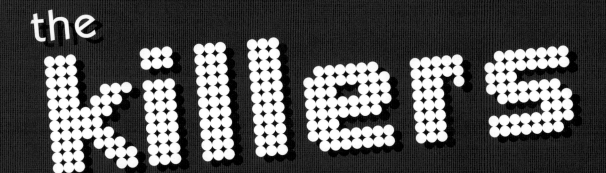

the killers

LAURA DOZIER

artnik books

SPECIAL THANKS...
www.killersmusic.com
www.lizardkingrecords.com
www.xtaster.co.uk
www.thekillers.amplifier.at
www.mrbrightside.com
www.nme.com
www.livejournal.com/community/_killmenow_
www.thekillers.stereooflies.com
www.thekillersonline.net
www.thekillersuk.com
www.killerscollection.co.uk
www.killers.homelinux.com

www.thekillersnetwork.com
www.thekillersontop.com
www.thekillersandme.piczo.com
www.thekillers.flirtatious.org
www.brandon.flirtatious.org
www.brandon-flowers.com
www.templeofmark.thekillersnetwork.com
www.shapemould.com
www.thekillers.sphosting.com
www.groups.msn.com/brandonflowersfansite
www.groups.msn.com/TheKillersOnline
www.fan.memories-fade.net/hotfuss
www.fan.metal-idol.net/all

www.andy.fan-cythis.com
www.velvet-angels.com/inmysoul
www.fan.canelinha.net/midnight
www.broken.forsaken-faith.org/songs.killers
www.killers.truedestinies.com
www.thekillers.de.tt
www.geocities.com/t4fs/killers.html
www.freewebs.com/amidnightshow/index.htm
www.vitaminrecords.com
www.isound.com
www.vh1.com
www.urbanoutfitters.com
www.laurenkent.com

In November 2003, squinting under the glare of the spotlights, Brandon Flowers scanned the overflowing audience at Tramps, the largest gay bar in Las Vegas. The crowd was peppered with transvestites, leather boyz, and gym bunnies – looking very butch indeed – but there were straights, too.

Like The Killers you don't have to be HOMOSEXUAL TO BE GAY.

Brandon scanned the crowd in vain for the groups of darkly clad nu-metal enthusiasts who typically clustered and stared intently at his band's bright, cheerful garb and their renditions of poppy, Eighties-inspired songs. They weren't there. Instead, the audience was attentive and met Brandon's sweeping gaze with cheers.

Clustered around the stage apron was a crowd of around 200 fans who had gathered just to see his band, The Killers. He felt butterflies in his stomach. He turned to the other members of the band. They had picked up on it too; but none of them really registered it. Or wanted to. Maybe it was starting to happen... but taking your Luck for granted might turn the Lady against you.

After all, they were Vegas boys.

They opened with 'Mr Brightside', which was to become their signature tune:

Jealousy
Turning saints into the sea
Swimming through sick lullabies
Choking on your alibis
But it's just the price I pay
Destiny is calling me
Open up my eager eyes
Cus I'm Mr. Brightside

The audience let rip and roared for an encore. The band felt the vibe: the promise of bigger things to come was as tangible as the cigarette smoke in the air. There were only around 200 in the crowd but it was still the largest gig that the band had ever played. As the lights dimmed, The Killers waved a feverish goodbye, ending their farewell performance at Tramps on a crystal-shattering high C. In the coming weeks, Brandon and the band, with this exhilarating gig under their belts, made the trip across the Atlantic to England, and began a tour that was to catapult them into rock'n'roll orbit.

LAS VEGAS
Birthplace of The Killers

Trespassing on the stomping ground of sequinned drag queens, Brandon Flowers pranced seductively across the stage at Tramps on Sundays in the summer of 2003. Although oozing sex-appeal and adorned with glitter, eyeliner and mascara, Brandon diverged from the standard Tramps performer at two crucial junctures: he wore flashy suits, not dresses, and refrained from belting out classic show tunes in a falsetto.

This front man of the recently formed band, The Killers, sang catchy, danceable rock 'n' roll with a sound created by rummaging through the pantheon of 80s' music gods: U2, New Order, The Cure, and Duran Duran.

But no matter how beguiling The Killers' look and familiar their sound seemed to be, Vegas is not known for cultivating young indie bands. In fact, most groups wither in the harsh desert soil after only a matter of months. The only band known to break out of Las Vegas had been Slaughter and, although the average person would blankly nod if told that bit of trivia, for aspiring local bands Slaughter's minor success story has become the stuff of legend.

The name The Killers was partly chosen because it chimed with Slaughter.

In 2003, Tramps, the favourite venue of The Killers, sat dwarfed by the colossal casinos and hotels that loomed in the distance. Located amongst a strip of gay bars, Tramps was wedged in the same seedy Vegas avenue as the smoky dive-bar the Double Down Saloon, which has been described by its owners as the 'anti-Vegas'.

Both of these Paradise Road establishments were anti-Vegas in the sense that they were planted firmly on the opposite side of the spectrum from the shiny Bellagios and Caesar's Palaces of the touristy, family-friendly Strip.

But if you consider Vegas to be **a mecca for the eccentric, flashy, and sexually liberated,** then Tramps and Double Down embodied Sin City to a T.

In addition to its vibrant gay scene, Paradise Road attracted goths, off-duty strippers, and blue-haired punks, forming a crowd with varied and often extreme musical tastes. To placate their cruisy clientele, both the Double Down and Tramps had band nights for the local talent.

Although on the eccentric side, underground music venues like Tramps offered the possibility of building a loyal, hometown following, which in Vegas is as enticing and elusive as reaching an oasis in the middle of the surrounding desert. Most of the town's venues cater for tourists, which means new local bands find it difficult to build either a fan base or an act. Nonetheless that doesn't stop lots trying.

HOUSE OF BLUES   BOX OFFICE
31 GOO GOO DOLLS   FRI 11PM FLASHBA
31 CRYSTAL METHOD   SAT 11PM BOOGIE KN
N 2 THE BANGLES   SUN 11PM JUICE
     EVERY SUNDAY GOSPEL BRUNCH 10 AM & 1 PM

In the cutthroat music arena of Vegas, securing a residency at Tramps was a coup for The Killers who were already accustomed to playing venues where the majority of the audience had come out to hear a completely different type of music. Performing after hard-metal groups to a less-than-receptive audience had led Brandon in particular to develop a larger-than-life stage persona, which actually did catch the eye of the fans of other music... well, for a while.

Generally Vegas is the final resting place for tried-and-true music veterans such as Elvis Presley and Frank Sinatra. Nowadays it is home to the likes of Celine Dion, Elton John and perma-tanned, slick-wigged crooners such as Wayne Newton, the quintessential Vegas act.

The constant turnover of tourists patronises these well-established artists and bands, who play at the casinos and larger venues like the House of Blues. Start-up bands can only play the fringe, which is why they usually don't last long and certainly never make it big.

This inhospitable environment has caused music journalists, musicians, and even the local fans to slate the Vegas music scene for everything from its lacklustre radio stations to the here-today-gone-tomorrow venues.

Tramps itself could not survive and closed last year. But, surprisingly, the curse of the Vegas music scene did not rear its ugly head and devour the fledgling group. Instead, when Brandon and the band became guest performers on Sundays – 80s' Night at Tramps – they developed a small but loyal fan base that eventually began to stir up some excitement in the local press.

The rumbling on the Vegas scene eventually spread and, while rejected by domestic labels such as the American powerhouse Warner Music, the Killers were signed up by a small UK record label, Lizard King, who booked the trip.

When they embarked on their UK tour, the odds were stacked against them hitting the jackpot but after that last gig in TRAMPS the band felt they were on a roll...

BABY KILLERS
Early life of the Band

On June 21, 1981, Brandon Flowers was born in Las Vegas; when he was 8 years old, his family moved to Nephi, Utah. Looking for a change of pace, his parents chose a very small town, named after the first book of the Mormon bible. Over eighty percent of Utah is Mormon and, in opposition to the decadent Sin City, Nephi more closely matched the devout Mormon family's religious preferences.

However, even at such an early age, Vegas seemed to have seized hold of Brandon, making him just a bit different. With a population of less than 5,000 people, Nephi offered the traditional small-town activities and conservative values of Middle America, and Brandon never quite fitted in.

'Brandon was probably the only Smiths fan in Nephi, period,' childhood friend Wyatt Boswell told **Rolling Stone**. 'It's a little farm town that thrives on football, so he was seen as a little off.'

'You play golf?
You listen to Elton John?
He caught a lot of shit for that.'

Brandon's unconventional music tastes and his aversion to football cemented his outsider status, but it was his chubbiness that compounded his insecurity. 'I was quite a porker when I was younger,' he admits. 'I never went swimming or anything like that because I didn't want anyone to see my body. I always assumed that people were looking at me... if I heard someone laughing, say in a restaurant, it would kill me.'

Bullied and teased because of his weight, Brandon feels the repercussions even today: 'It gave me a terrible sense of self-image, and I guess I carry that around with me still.'

...ow, Brandon steps on stage to the frenzied screams of utterly besotted girls (and boys), boasting a thin physique. 'It's not anorexia, though,' Flowers says, defensively. 'But I am weight-conscious, absolutely.'

Yet, despite his overwhelming sex appeal and popularity, Brandon's childhood insecurities have affected his song writing and even his stage presence. The homosexual undertones in The Killers' music and Brandon's effeminate stage presence stem more from Utah, the locale of Brandon's childhood, than the typical scapegoat, Vegas. After all, it was in Utah where Brandon grew up as a young boy, divided from his peers by his interests and his appearance.

During school, Brandon always wanted to perform in the theatre, but his lack of confidence got in the way. 'I was really shy on stage. I still have stage fright up until today. But the more we perform, the easier it gets. You have to be very confident to play for 5,000 people, you know,' he explained in 2005. Obviously Brandon has overcome his childhood fear.

But how did he manage to conquer his demons? A clue exists in his stage persona.

An interviewer once asked Brandon if dressing up and putting on make-up helped him deal with his insecurity. Flowers answered: 'Perhaps it is like putting on a mask. All the way down to the jackets and the vests. They're all extra layers that I can put on.' The distinctly feminine dance moves, pink jackets and eyeliner are all part of a mask that allows him to battle against his former lack of self-confidence.

Brandon's affinity with the mask of make-up began when he was only thirteen, when he was struggling with his less-than-perfect appearance. At a Cure concert with his older brother, Brandon donned eyeliner for the first time. Remembering with pleasure, Brandon laughed and said, 'I thought I looked very cool.' And since that day, make-up for Brandon has been tied to rock 'n' roll and the hip mien of a rock star. His attraction to its transformative powers appears in full force as he steps on stage with The Killers; after all, he never performs without it.

As Brandon began experimenting with make-up, he was also on the cusp of an obsession with a boy who attended his school. Brandon was a loner in Utah, which spurred him towards some tortured hero worship of the big man on campus.

He has encapsulated this troubled period in one of his songs, 'Andy You're a Star', where he sings about an intense attraction to a fellow student. Mentioning lockers, a football game and 'parking', the song channels the atmosphere of a typical American school, but the innocent backdrop is rife with anguished repression and unrequited desire.

Brandon sings with heartrending longing:

In a car with a girl, promise me
She's not your world
Cause Andy, you're a star
In nobody's eyes but mine.

As for the actual identity of Andy, Brandon has always been coy about giving any clues to the real person behind the unusual, intriguing song. In an interview with **The Times** he hedged: 'I'm not sure I should tell you who Andy is. 'He was my friend in eighth grade: a football player and the popular kid. If you're the loner, there are always going to be people that you want to be, even if it's just for one day.'

More homoerotic than a Greek bathhouse, 'Andy' undeniably portrays homosexual longing. However, when asked about the gay elements in his work, Brandon skirts around the issue, trying to leave the song and his personal motives open to interpretation: 'I want people to make our songs their own.

'That's the beauty of art. So many people have so many opinions of what songs mean. That's really my motive. I would never write a song for just one type of person. The fact that both jocks and gays come to our shows proves that it's working.'

Besides the universal appeal, this homosexual
edge has given the band an added layer of intrigue,
something to differentiate it from the hoards of of other
wannabes. Of course, Brandon's sexual ambiguity is a big issue
with the fans, who want to know whether he is bi-sexual or not. He
always plays with his answers. In one interview he gave to *Boyz* in early
2005, he gave a fairly definitive answer but tinged it with a coyness that left
one wondering whether he was being truthful:

Vegas must have a seedy side too?
Yeah, there are areas where there are gangs, and the prostitution and everything, definitely.

Did you ever get caught up in all that?
No. Never had a hooker!

You're a big hit with gay indie gentlemen, were you aware of that?
I assumed that.

Why, do you get a lot of boyz throwing themselves at you?
Er, sometimes, yeah.

How do you feel about it?
Well, we're here for boys and girls. We don't turn anybody away!

Ever gone there?
Er, no. Not yet.

So do you think the fact that you're hot helps you sell records?
I just think it's the whipped cream.

Whipped cream?
Yeah, whipped cream on top. The Killers are the pie and I guess the looks are the cherry.

Do you find the debauchery side of things tempting?
Yeah, absolutely. Every night!

And have you resisted temptation every time?
I've got a really good ratio.

Of good behaviour versus bad behaviour?
Yeah, exactly!

So have there been groupies back to the hotel room, that kind of thing?
Erm... Not mine.

But some of the other band members have?
Maybe...

Did you ever get it on with one of those TRAMPS transsexuals?
[laughs] No!

Not even by accident?
No, there weren't any that were that pretty!

Then, in August 2005, Brandon
spoiled his cagey game by
getting married!

After leaving Utah behind, Brandon went to live in Las Vegas at the age of 16 and began to attend Chaparral High School. He continued playing golf and even toyed with the idea of becoming a professional player, copying the aspirations of his older brother. In fact, Brandon has described his brother, Shane, as one of the major driving forces in his life:

'He was way cooler and very handsome, the kind of guy who got to go to the prom with Miss Nevada. He was the reason I got into golf, and then music. Everything Shane did, I wanted to do too.'

Twelve years Brandon's senior, Shane listened to the Cars, the Beatles, Morrissey and The Cure, and this cool big brother transformed his eager sibling into a music connoisseur and an out-and-out anglophile. 'American stuff such as Korn and Nirvana always sounded like trash to me,' Brandon confessed.

The Cars were one of his favourites: 'I bought *Greatest Hits* when I was 12. It was really weird because other kids were buying Tool and Nirvana and I was buying the Cars and the Psychedelic Furs.

I WAS PRETTY ALIENATED AS A KID.'

In response to his alienation, Brandon turned inward, looking to his family for companionship and his family's religion for guidance. **Rolling Stone** Magazine has covered how family, faith and Utah played such a huge role in Brandon's development. In a 2004 interview with the band, the magazine outlined the Flowers' family history and quoted him on the relevance of Nephi as a town name: 'The Book of Nephi is the first book in the Book of Mormon. It begins: "I, Nephi, having been born of goodly parents, therefore I was taught somewhat in the learning of my father."'

While their town name actually proclaimed the wisdom of following the examples of the older generation, Flowers' father and grandfather before him were produce men, working in grocery stores.

Another more all-encompassing tradition was the mission trip. When Mormon males turn nineteen, they leave for a two-year mission to seek converts. Flowers' older brother went to Chile. 'My whole life, I thought I would do it too.'

In other words, the older generation and the examples set forth by one's ancestors had great significance for the Flowers' family. Following in the footsteps of his older brother, Brandon assumed the musical tastes and golfing habits of his idol, already revealing a talent for mimicry.

Avoiding the American music of his peers, Brandon would sneak into Shane's room to watch music videos of U2 and stare at his thrilling band posters. The Cure's 'The Head on The Door' poster, with the band splashed in face paint, particularly stands out in his memory. Shane also directed Brandon to one of his primary musical influences, Morrissey, which eventually led Brandon to branch out on his own to explore David Bowie.

'I'd read about Bowie in Morrissey interviews, but it never prompted me to buy his records. I specifically remember the day I got out of a math class in college and heard 'Changes' on the radio.

I loved it. Now Ziggy Stardust and Hunky Dory are my babies,' said Flowers.

Brandon's musical interest originally derived from his brother. However, the seductive power of music eventually supplanted the . After he finished high school in Las Vegas, Brandon broke his habit of brother worship and religious devotion by avoiding his mission trip. As religion and family became secondary, Brandon came to adopt a very different set of icons – musicians.

He came to respect artists such as Oasis, U2, and New Order, which have undeniably influenced his songwriting; many Killers songs have riffs and melodies distinctly reminiscent of his heroes. Yet in these allusions traces of his Mormon roots remain, for as the town name, Nephi, resonates with the Mormon philosophy, so it corresponds with Brandon's musical agenda. The Mormon respect for one's elders has translated into an almost pious obsession with the English musical greats of the 80s and early 90s.

After school, Brandon's musical interests hardened into ambition. He met a caddy at a Vegas golf course with similar taste in music, and the two started a synth band known as Blush Response. For the first time, Brandon turned his hand towards writing songs.

Necessity is the mother of invention, and so the songs developed around the poppy, artificial **sound of a keyboard,** the only instrument Brandon could play.

PJ Perez, a Vegas musician and one of the earliest reviewers of The Killers for the *Las Vegas Weekly*, bluntly expressed Blush Response's status in Vegas: 'I know Flowers talks about being in a synth group called Blush Response, but nobody I know ever recalls seeing them play.'

In effect, they were nobodies. Scrambling to make a blip on the radar screen of rock'n'roll air traffic, Blush Response decided to leave Las Vegas for LA, but Brandon declined to go with it.

Although Brandon's first foray into the music industry spluttered to a temporary halt, his experience in Blush Response incited his interest in forming a band and in songwriting. He also discovered the limits of synth pop. After all, the tangy, frivolous sound of Blush Response had failed to make even a dent in the Vegas scene.

After attending an Oasis concert, Brandon decided his music needed a more organic sound, a sound driven by guitars in particular. Nonetheless, *Hot Fuss*, The Killers' debut album, is pumped more full of synth riffs and hooks than a Vegas slot machine is fed quarters. However, he has added depth to the synthetic sound of Blush Response by layering in rock drumming and sinuous guitar lines.

GOLD COAST

PARKING
-ENTRANCE-

HONKY TONK ANGELS
SPECIAL GUEST MALE TRIBUTES TO
ALAN JACKSON & CHARLIE DANIELS
OCT. 24 - NOV. 4

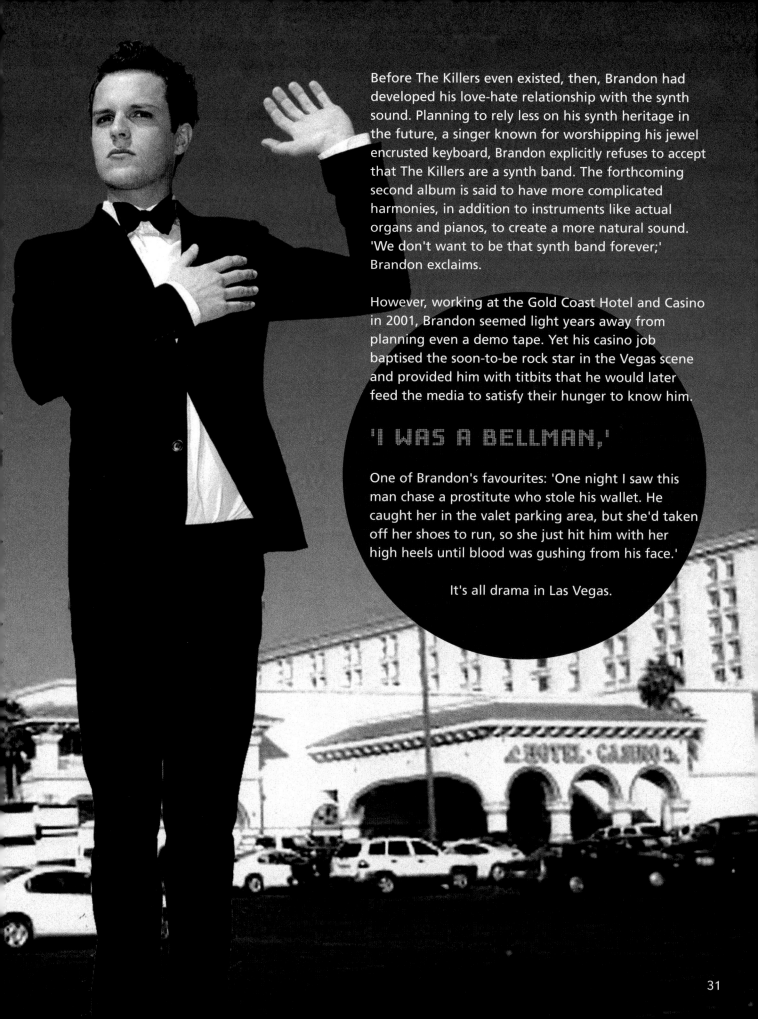

Before The Killers even existed, then, Brandon had developed his love-hate relationship with the synth sound. Planning to rely less on his synth heritage in the future, a singer known for worshipping his jewel encrusted keyboard, Brandon explicitly refuses to accept that The Killers are a synth band. The forthcoming second album is said to have more complicated harmonies, in addition to instruments like actual organs and pianos, to create a more natural sound. 'We don't want to be that synth band forever;' Brandon exclaims.

However, working at the Gold Coast Hotel and Casino in 2001, Brandon seemed light years away from planning even a demo tape. Yet his casino job baptised the soon-to-be rock star in the Vegas scene and provided him with titbits that he would later feed the media to satisfy their hunger to know him.

'I WAS A BELLMAN,'

One of Brandon's favourites: 'One night I saw this man chase a prostitute who stole his wallet. He caught her in the valet parking area, but she'd taken off her shoes to run, so she just hit him with her high heels until blood was gushing from his face.'

It's all drama in Las Vegas.

LAS VEGAS
WEEKLY.

Bass, electronic drums, keys,
strings. Ages 18-33 pref. Influences:
Radiohead, Bjork, Beatles, Foo
Fighters. ▓▓▓▓▓▓▓
▓▓▓▓▓▓▓
june 2001

BASS PLAYER NEEDED- Drowning
▓▓▓▓▓▓▓ call 312-4422 or
▓▓6-0702

Bass Player and Drummer needed for
all original band. Influences: Oasis,
Smashing Pumpkins, Bowie,
Radiohead ▓▓▓▓▓ *july 2001*
▓▓▓▓▓▓▓▓▓▓

Bass Player and Drummer needed
immediately for blues, influ▓▓▓
▓▓▓▓ Growe▓▓▓ 30-35 or
younger. (702) 212-1259

Singer/songwriter/guitarist forming original band. Need: bass,
keys, electronic drums, viola,
cello etc. Infl: Beatles, Bjork,
Radiohead, Beck, Sunny Day
Real estate. 3▓▓▓▓
▓▓▓▓▓▓ *Sept 2001*

Vocalist Frontman wanted for Punk /
Metal▓▓▓▓▓ 24-34▓▓▓▓▓▓
▓▓▓▓▓▓▓▓▓▓▓▓▓▓▓▓▓▓
20-28. No drugs. Call Ben 658-2776

Bass Player and Drummer Wanted, age
19-30, needed for all original band.
Influences: Smashing Pumpkins, the
Strokes, New Order, Ben Folds, Depeche
Mode. ▓▓▓▓▓ *Dec 2001*

▓▓▓▓ guitarist from San Bernardino,
▓▓▓▓▓▓▓▓▓▓▓▓▓▓▓▓▓▓
▓▓▓▓▓▓▓ tui. ▓▓▓
August 2002 @ 806-3825

Bass player needed for rock band.
All original music, influences: the
Cure, Rolling Stones, David Bowie
and New order. ph. ▓▓▓▓▓▓

Bass player needed for the Killers:
check out
www.lvlocalmusicscene.com for more
info. ph. ▓▓▓▓▓▓
sept 2002   Covers and ori▓

But when Brandon wasn't toting the luggage of tourists and watching the occasional prostitute slip into the elevator, he focused on music. Left stranded without a band in the summer of 2001, Brandon had to resort to drastic measures – the classified section. Whether looking for a lover or a band to join, newspaper classifieds are notorious for pulling in the weirdos. However, Brandon just happened to read and respond to an ad placed by Dave Keuning.

When the two met, it was like LOVE AT FIRST SIGHT.

Well, almost... 'Brandon was the only person to reply to my ad who wasn't a complete freak,' Keuning states matter-of-factly. And although Brandon did not have much competition, the creative chemistry between the two musicians clicked immediately. 'He came over with his keyboard and we started going through song ideas straight away. I had the verse to "Mr. Brightside" and he went away and wrote the chorus. That was the first song we wrote together and remains the only song that we've played at every single Killers show,' Keuning remembers.

Dave had moved to Las Vegas from Pella, Iowa in January 2001, and he had been looking to start a band upon his arrival. He had placed several ads in the Las Vegas Weekly before meeting Brandon.

Feeling bored and stifled by the limited possibilities of Pella, Dave had decided to leave his small hometown. Pella, similar to Nephi, is a traditional and rather insular community, where most of the excitement centres on football and its Dutch roots. The town even named the mascot of the high school football team the Flying Dutchman. In addition to the Dutch bakeries and shops, there are festivals that celebrate the town's heritage. In fact, Dave walked in the Tulip Time parade every year in the traditional wooden clogs until he was in the sixth grade.

But Dave needed more excitement than football and the clog walking parade.

Born on 28 March 1976, Dave discovered music early and started learning the guitar at age fourteen. Aerosmith, AC/DC and the rest of the classic rock canon ignited his passion for guitar, and these 'bands you'd be into when

you're going through puberty' as K
has termed them, have influenced h

'He was pretty determined to try an
master guitar,' said his father, Chuck Keuning. 'Of course, like most paren
had no idea he would carry it this far
'I just always could hear him practicin
his room,' said his mother. 'We kind o
that; it's kind of quiet in the house no

After taking some guitar lessons, Dave
joined the Pella High School jazz band
sophomore, and this experience gave h
greater technical skill. He learned to re
music, and jazz exposed him to a differe
style and a greater range of chords than
his typical diet of rock music provided.
Even today, Dave remembers with pleasu
how when he was a member the school
band won state championships.

Greetings from Pella
IOWA

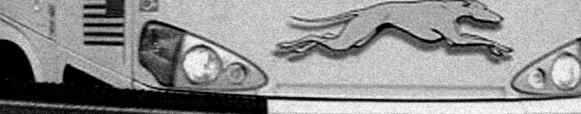

7135

7135

LAS VEGAS

WELCOME TO

KIRKWOOD
COMMUNITY COLLEGE

At the same time, Dave also played with a Newton-based Christian rock band called Pickle for about four years. Pickle's band members, Keith Nester and Kyle Reynolds, first met Keuning in 1993. 'He was just like a monster on guitar at this early age,' Nester said. Reynolds agreed, 'He always had a real knack for coming up with original riffs and original arrangements to songs.'

Although PICKLE was key for his musical development, Keuning claimed that he never termed himself a 'Christian ROCKER'.

Interestingly, the religious background of both Keuning and Flowers has affected their music and now, in the limelight, both try to distance themselves from any religious tag.

'It was cool to be part of something positive,' Keuning has said, carefully avoiding linking himself with any religious agenda. 'They were great musicians. They helped me get better. They taught me a lot of new things.'

In 1995 he enrolled in Kirkwood Community College and then attended the University of Iowa. However, Dave eventually dropped out and began to scramble around for a new course of action. Keuning's parents, Sandy and Chuck, owned a plumbing and air-conditioning service, and Dave always had the option to stay and join the family business. Instead he decided to leave for Las Vegas, hoping for inspiration from that most barren of places – Vegas, the city known for being a cultural desert.

After the move he bided his time, waiting for something to happen while working as a sales assistant at the clothing store Banana Republic. Yet from this rather bleak pitstop, Dave did eventually find what he was looking for – a chance to play in a band. After a year, Dave met Brandon, and they formed an early version of The Killers, performing regular gigs in a Vegas dive bar.

'It had a lot of space in it, couches and stuff,' Keuning remembered.

'Bums would sleep on the couches sometimes, and no one would kick 'em out. The place was open 'til 6 or 7 in the morning.'

Still serving during the day at the clothing store, Dave managed to put in some piece-work as a rock-star bad-boy. He allegedly had got into the habit of luring girls into the dressing rooms for groupie sex. We can be sure that, if it occurred, the sex was consensual and with no one under age. Dave, like the rest of the band, is a good boy first and a break-every-rule rock 'n' roller last. The Killers don't fuck up. They work hard and will always stop playing hard at the point where it interferes with their work.

Drugs? No drugs, of course... well, maybe some grass. The Killers hint at trying out marijuana but even then the reporter is left thinking such admissions are made to preserve some kind of rock credibility. A squeaky-clean rock 'n' roller is, after all, a contradiction in terms.

Nevertheless, it was from this grungy dive that the founding members of The Killers would materialise. At this time – summer 2000 – there was no Ronnie Vannucci and Mark Stoermer. The band had a different bass player, Dell Star, 18, and drummer, the 30-something Buss Bradley. These two less-than-adept members were quickly dismissed and Keuning began advertising for replacements as early as September of that year.

A venerable Vegas music critic observed: 'I don't think anybody on the local scene was surprised when Dave and Brandon brought the others in to replace Dell Star and Buss Bradley – they didn't click and were holding The Killers back.'

Ronnie Vannucci Jr., the drummer, joined first. Born on 15 February 1976 in Las Vegas, Ronnie describes himself as 'one of those service industry kids'. His family was entrenched in the tourism-driven economy of Vegas; Ronnie's mum worked as a cocktail waitress and his dad as a bartender in Caesar's Palace.

Ronnie described his unusual hometown as a constant buzz of activity: 'It's 24 hours. It's accessible. You can have anything you want any time.' And like this all-night city, his life was far from the standard 9-to-5. His parents often worked until 4am, and this unusual schedule translated to him: they never even batted an eye when he strolled in past midnight.

With his very Vegas upbringing, he also had a good helping of music. His father introduced him to a wide variety of tunes, from the Beatles to jazz. But one album had particular influence on the young Vannucci; he relished every note of the first tape he ever bought, 'The Head on the Door' by The Cure, which eventually made his interests harmonise perfectly with Flowers and the rest of The Killers.

What particularly attracted Ronnie was rhythm, and he developed an all-encompassing passion for the intoxicating beat of rock songs:

'I'd lock myself in the garage and beat on the washer and dryer and fridge; out in the garage, just for hours on end,' said Vannucci. 'I would do that in lieu of riding bikes with friends or something.' And he even followed this passion for rhythm in his studies; after attending Western High School, he studied for and received a degree in percussion from UNLV.

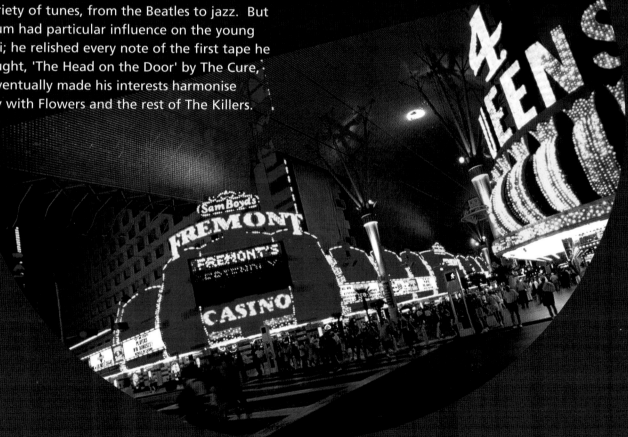

While at university, Ronnie moonlighted at the Little Chapel of Flowers as a photographer. Perhaps one of the classier chapels on the Strip (after all, Britney Spears graced its altar for her first wedding), this Vegas wedding venue still has all the expected bells and whistles of the theme churches that dot the city. Upon request a lookalike Elvis, Tom Jones or Prince can attend the lucky couple's ceremony. As one might expect, Ronnie has a collection of strange stories from this job.

Recounting one of the most eccentric weddings that he experienced, Vannucci said, 'There was this one couple. They were both attorneys and they actually had a mock jury and were sentenced to life with each other. **They even had handcuffs. It got a little kinky and it got a little weird... I think they were planning on physically consummating their marriage on the altar. The Registrar put the dampeners on that.'**

Not destined for a life of recording such bizarre couplings, Ronnie received a phone call while sitting at the lake near UNLV, and a friend asked him if he could fill in on the drums for a band called The Killers.

As luck would have it, he agreed.

The final band member, Mark Stoermer, had to be coerced into joining. At first reluctant to leave his current band because he played with several close friends, Mark eventually agreed and the new version of The Killers started practicing in that time-honoured start-up locale, the garage.

Born 28 June 1981, Mark is the second youngest band member behind Brandon. Another Las Vegas local, Mark grew up listening to a very different genre of music than the other members. Rap was the music that initially entranced the young Stoermer. 'I got Public Enemy's **Yo! Bum Rush The Show** when I was ten and I loved it! I loved the noises on it,' he recently admitted. In fact, this trumpet player-turned guitarist did not actively listen to rock until he heard Nirvana.

Tall – around 6'3" – this deadpan bass player cuts an intimidating, hulking figure that smoulders with a mysterious aura on stage, but it isn't too hard to imagine this severe, reserved character lost in a pile of text books either.

Like Vannucci, Mark attended UNLV, but despite his musical interests, he never planned on making a career from his hobby. He studied philosophy and had more practical plans like becoming 'a lawyer or college professor or something academic.'

In 2002, when the band formed, Mark worked as a medical courier, transporting blood, the occasional body part, and boxers' samples for post-fight drug testing. Although not the glamorous gig he would soon acquire, Mark did have a sniff of star-power from the driver's seat – once he delivered the urine of the then Heavyweight World Champion Lennox Lewis. And this odd job had other benefits as well.

Driving for hours, he had time to bone up on rock music 'It was basically a driver job with a CD player, so it allowed me to discover a lot of music,' he explained. In addition to The Cure, U2 and New Order, Stoermer drove his medical van to the sounds of bassists such as Noel Redding of the Jimi Hendrix Experience, The Who's Pete Townsend, and Paul McCartney.

Mark is mostly a pick player, and his distinctive sound developed during his medical van tutelage.

'I LOVE THE PUNCH AND GRIT OF A PICK,'

said Stoermer in an early 2005 interview, 'and that comes a lot from McCartney. I do a lot of unconscious palm muting. I love how you can instantly get that clunky tone with shorter notes. It's a great sound.'

A Killer Reception: MAKING IT BIG

When a bellhop, a medical courier, a wedding photographer, and a lusty Banana Republic employee get together and play music, you would expect the audience to laugh rather than dance. However, Flowers, Keuning, Vannucci and Stoermer were *sui generis* – from the beginning The Killers were greater than the sum of their individual parts. That was partly because they worked so hard.

The eclectic group began to practice in Ronnie's uncle's sweltering garage, with temperatures often well over 100°F. Vannucci occasionally managed to sneak them into UNLV for late-night practice sessions as well, which was cooler and prevented Ronnie from having to lug around his drums. The band also took every opening to play live – really this was just an extension of their harrowing practice routine. It was usually unpaid, too; but they were developing a repertoire and an act. The reviews were not that great but a few low-circulation Vegas giveaways marked them as a band to watch. Even then, The Killers were seen by some Vegas music critics as a group that could emulate Slaughter.

Doggedly playing the tough dive-bar circuit paid off, however. They gelled and developed a professional act much quicker than most bands. Then, with only a modest following, they managed to attract a manager and the attention of an English record label, Lizard King, who invited them to tour the UK. Leaving Las Vegas opened up new horizons, and the band's decision to depart both their hometown and the U.S. proved to be a critical turning point in their success story.

The band took a week off from their day jobs for their November 2003 tour. Yet the venues remained dingy and initally their performances did not attract the industry scouts. But in the music business things can turn around fast. 'They played places like the Camden Barfly, which are essentially pubs,' explained Siona Ryan, a Lizard King exec. The Barfly is a hotspot for debuting bands that become household names. Ryan remembered, 'Being so early in their career, it was mainly industry heads who were at the gigs, including quite a few A&R people who weren't sure if they were signed or not.'

Ben Durling, the Lizard King A&R man who had made the decision to sign the group, recalled why: 'The first two songs I heard were "Mr Brightside" and "Somebody Told Me" and they weren't too dissimilar to what's on the record so I thought it was a pretty obvious thing at the time.

'The whole '80s revival was starting to rear its head in the UK and The Killers were potentially a perfect fit. Bands like The Strokes and The White Stripes had also made it cool to be American again, so the timing felt really right.'

One thing was for sure, the Vegas band were not casino crooners and Durling's judgement was soon to be vindicated.

The label signed the band based solely on a five-track demo, which included: 'Mr Brightside', 'Somebody Told Me', 'On Top', 'Smile Like You Mean It' and 'Who Let You Go'.

Soon after returning to the US, the band headed into the studio to record their first album, **Hot Fuss**, with Green Day manager Jeff Saltzman acting as producer. After the success of the album, The Killers down-played his influence and emphasised their own production savvy, claiming that there was very little input from him.

'We gave him credit, but we constructed all the songs and mostly did everything ourselves,' Ronnie Vannucci has insisted.

'There wasn't a lot of production involved. It was almost like a live show or rehearsal. No song was more than three takes.'

On the other hand, The Killers do acknowledge the significant contribution of the sound engineer Alan Moulder. 'He's worked with all our favourite bands,' Dave Keuning enthused. 'He's worked with not only the Smashing Pumpkins, but Depeche Mode. He's even worked with The Smiths – he engineered "Shoplifters Of The World Unite" – and he did Nine Inch Nails. They're not a huge influence on us, but that was one of the deciding facts, the way he did NIN's **The Fragile**. The sounds are so great on it, they're so loud. It's a great mix and that was a big deal for us.'

Of course, the album included more than the demo five songs that secured them the record deal. 'All These Things That I've Done', written after the first EP release, was an unexpected bonus for the album, stirring up crowds in concert after concert. Lizard King had booked them into Glastonbury 2004 but the organisers of the event slotted them into the New Bands venue, not the main stage.

The Killers had been typecast as the retro-New Wave sounds of New York City. Lizard King's Siona Ryan peddled their new-Millennium rock snarl and glitzy glam-rock but the festival bookers were not convinced – they stayed New Band.

Glastonbury 2004 proved the strength of the soon-to-be single, as the band electrified the crowd with the song's nostalgic sentiment and the rousing chant of

'I'VE GOT SOUL BUT I'M NOT A SOLDIER'

In fact, the band's success at Glastonbury marked their eruption on the UK music scene.

Siona didn't know what to expect at Glastonbury, but the performance blew her doubts out of the water. 'I'd hoped it was going to be a wow, but didn't know for sure until about 20 minutes beforehand when we were backstage and saw thousands and thousands of people beelining for the New Bands Tent, which was a bit out of the way,' she recalled. 'We were looking at each other thinking, "No, no, no!" I'm not joking, the crowd outside was probably 80 people deep and left the moment The Killers finished. I remember Ronnie and Brandon laughing at us afterwards because we were so overwhelmed. The word of mouth had really tipped over.'

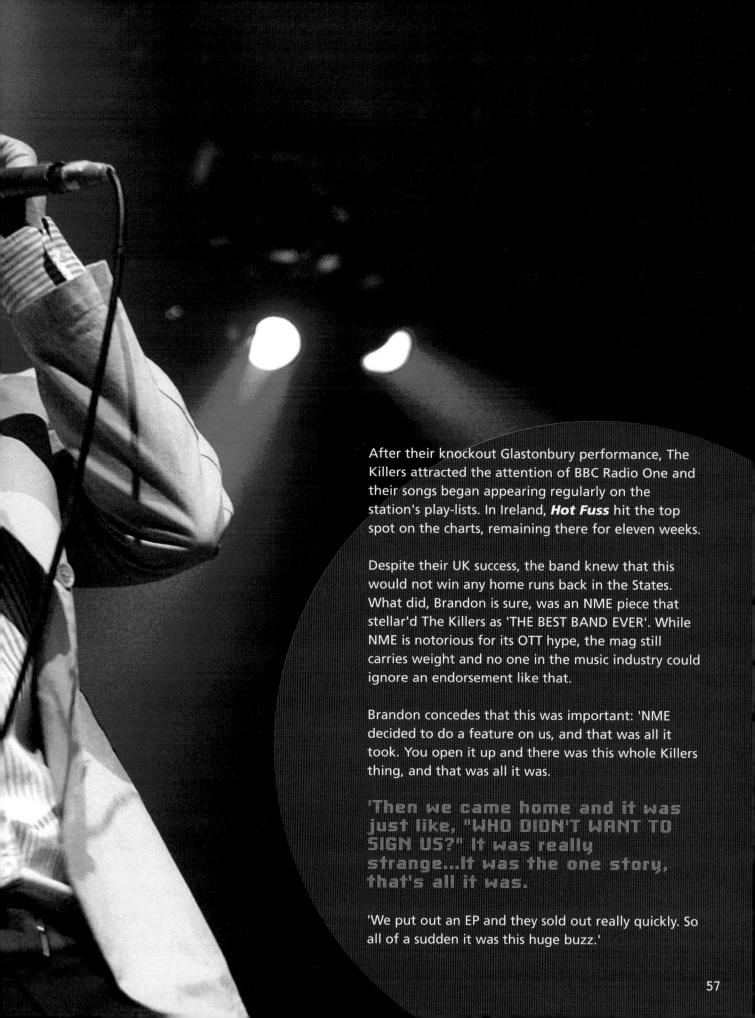

After their knockout Glastonbury performance, The Killers attracted the attention of BBC Radio One and their songs began appearing regularly on the station's play-lists. In Ireland, **Hot Fuss** hit the top spot on the charts, remaining there for eleven weeks.

Despite their UK success, the band knew that this would not win any home runs back in the States. What did, Brandon is sure, was an NME piece that stellar'd The Killers as 'THE BEST BAND EVER'. While NME is notorious for its OTT hype, the mag still carries weight and no one in the music industry could ignore an endorsement like that.

Brandon concedes that this was important: 'NME decided to do a feature on us, and that was all it took. You open it up and there was this whole Killers thing, and that was all it was.

'Then we came home and it was just like, "WHO DIDN'T WANT TO SIGN US?" It was really strange...It was the one story, that's all it was.

'We put out an EP and they sold out really quickly. So all of a sudden it was this huge buzz.'

With their rep hallmarked in England as platinum, the bigger American labels came a-courting. Island Records (Def Jam's sister label at Universal Music) signed them, but Island had some work to do. In the States, The Killers were an unknown indie group from Vegas but, with the music heavies on their side, they had the clout to hit the indifferent, inattentive US heartland. Their songs were played more frequently on the radio, the band began appearing on magazine covers, and they even landed a spot on the Tonight Show.

However, the band's appearance on Fox-TV's show **The O.C.** marked the beginning of widespread, mainstream American recognition.

With their *O.C.* appearance, The Killers became a household name.

The O.C. has been instrumental in the rejuvenation of indie-rock. Some purist Indie-bands turn their noses up at playing a sitcom in which rich teenagers at high school make-out, fight, and wear fashionable clothes. At first glance, it hardly seems like a platform for cool musicians. However, the characters also allude to hip music and, then , end up making-out/fighting to a soundtrack of chart-breaking songs.

The musical acumen of the producers and the characters, in addition to the extreme publicity that this popular show offers, have lured a continuous stream of premier acts like Franz Ferdinand, Modest Mouse and Beck. Then the show's soundtrack CDs, dotted with up-and-coming hits, sell like the latest *Harry Potter*. The show's first soundtrack sold over 63,000 copies in the United States.

The O.C. was an opportunity for us to get more people into our music. That's always a positive thing, as far as I am concerned,' Mark Stoermer admits slightly defensively.

Of course, like a lot of Vegas residents, the four Killers are CLUED-UP on playing the odds.

They knew they were on a roll but how long it was going to last was in the lap of the gods, and the rule in these circumstances is: cash in some chips early and don't chase your luck with the rest. *The O.C.* offer was like a card dealt off the bottom the pack. No real gambler looks askance at those.

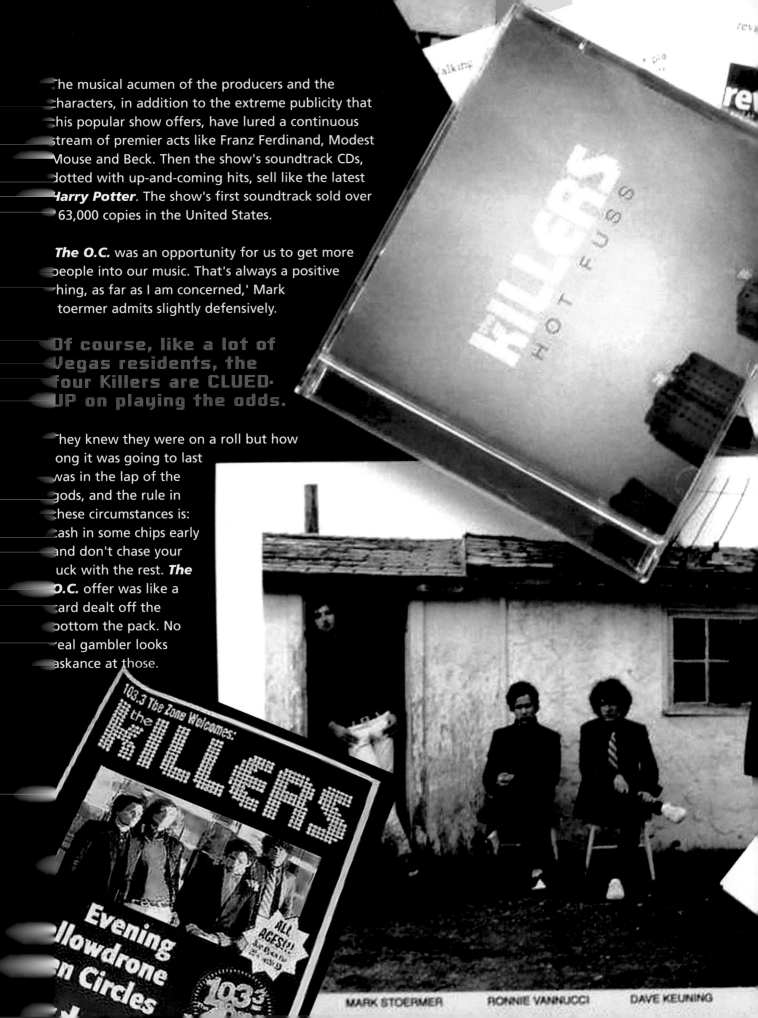

MARK STOERMER   RONNIE VANNUCCI   DAVE KEUNING

Once the money started to wash in, The Killers took to managing it like a duck to water. A lot of groups are too dazzled by the fame to watch that they get the fortune, too. It happens all the time: by default the agents, managers, accountants and record companies take the lion's share. That hasn't happened to The Killers. The cardinal sin with the hardcore followers of indie-rock bands is if their group – when it begins to break though – sells out to appeal to the mainstream. Although they were certainly trying to penetrate the American heartland, when they did *The O.C.* show in December 2004, they didn't sell out their act in the show's fictional venue, the Bait Shop. They worked 'Mr. Brightside', 'Smile Like You Mean It' and 'Everything Will Be Alright' just the way they always do.

What's all the Fuss about?: THE ALBUM

Hot Fuss was released in the UK on 7 June 2004 and a week later in the US. The pulsating, puffed-up rock arena sound of 'Somebody Told Me' and the soaring, poetic encapsulation of jealousy in 'Mr. Brightside' had incited some well-deserved hype. Music critics and fans alike had awaited the release of the album with nail-biting anticipation.

Hot Fuss delivered in spades. The band's earlier songs and performances always had an edge of decadence, *Hot Fuss* cranked up a sleazier, unapologetic campness packaged with mesmeric beats and intriguing lyrics.

The album indulges in a decidedly frivolous and unreal mood that resonates with the unabashed kitsch of their hometown. As one journalist pointed out, the consciously inauthentic has advantages:

'Artificiality doesn't cripple a fledgling band in our screw-it-all era. In fact, it's probably a huge selling point.'

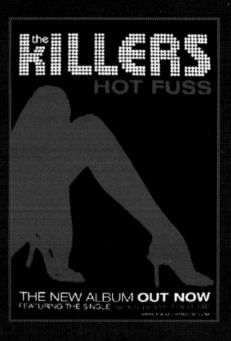

The blazing single 'Mr. Brightside' expresses the overwhelming jealousy of a paranoid boyfriend who terms himself, ironically, Mr. Brightside. The souped-up keyboards and evocative imagery of the lyrics conjure up the irrational self-torture of the green-eyed monster with tragi-comic pathos:

And I'm falling asleep
And she's calling a cab
While he's having a smoke
And she's taking a drag

And they're going to bed
And my stomach is sick
And its all in my head
But she's touching his chest
Now, he takes off her dress
Now, let me go.

'Somebody Told Me' has a huge sound with chunky riffs that manages to articulate a tongue-twisting, gender-bending situation of androgynous confusion and desire:

Well somebody told me
You had a boyfriend
Who looks like a girlfriend
That I had in February of
last year.

The song resonates with their sets at Tramps, where the flock of trannies and trans weren't, according to Brandon, pretty enough to get it on with.

Brandon in particular enthuses about 'Somebody told Me': 'I love the play on words. I think of it as a great icebreaker. I think of it as the ultimate pick-up line. If I was a girl I would think that it's very clever, if a boy came up to me and said that to me. It's our most light-hearted, most Las Vegas song. It's good, clean fun.'

And he's right, but the other tracks on **Hot Fuss** play to the darker end of the emotional spectrum.

'Believe Me Natalie', for instance, pleads with a Studio 54 AIDs victim to find before she dies a dance of death. It reeks of the mania that the 14th century victims of the Black Death embraced:

Believe me, Natalie
Listen Natalie
This is your last chance to find
A go-go dance to disco now.

The serpentine beat and the Cure-inspired synth reverie is a frantic, nostalgic tribute to fading youth and a dying era of music.

But good, clean fun it's not.

According to which side of the Atlantic the purchaser is on, the eleven tracks of the album differ slightly. The UK version includes the pummelling rhythms of 'Glamorous Indie Rock 'n' Roll', thankfully both had 'On Top' – The Killers' prophetic tribute to fame.

In that song Brandon sings:

We're on top
We bring the bump to the grind, uh huh
I don't mind, we're on top
It's just a shimmy and a shake, uh huh.

Foreshadowing the top-dog position of Brandon's band, this danceable record would go on to sell over 2 million copies. The lyrics of 'On Top' have a clever take on the transience of fame and how you should enjoy it while you can without taking it too seriously. Anyone looking for a philosophy behind The Killers' work need look no further.

Musically, Brandon vamps up the synth in his anthemic stadium rock style, while Vannucci and Keuning drive the rhythm section along like a herd of stampeding buffalo. The song climaxes in Mark Stoermer's crescendo of guitar play, which pays tribute to one of his own idols, Jimi Hendrix.

The suave slickness of the songs has led some to criticise the album as over-produced. However, nothing could be further from the truth. This double-platinum record developed from garage practices and apartment recording sessions. 'A little over half the record is the demo. We just made it to let people have a listen but it turned out good, so we decided to release it. There's a freshness to it and, on some level, a lot of spontaneity,' claimed Keuning.

Brandon penned the indulgently melancholy 'Everything Will Be Alright' and then the band actually recorded it in Keuning's apartment. Adding the guitar and some 'weird noises' (as Keuning described them), they captured this musical gem on the spur of a moment.

Keuning remembered the problems:

'We tried in a fancier studio to redo that one, but it just sounded like crap. IT SOUNDED TOO SLICK.

'You'd think it would be easier, but there was some kind of weird magic. It was a 16-track recorder. Nothing professional, but good enough.'

The Killers mastered the production crafts of recording very quickly. They are truly a band that does everything it can to manage its own output. Some might say they are control freaks, others might prefer to call them perfectionists.

Brandon directs much of the songwriting but the other three contribute, in varying degrees, to the creation of the band's music. It's a fairly disorganised process, often instigated when one of them get an idea or inspiration.

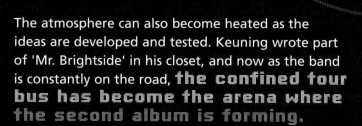

The atmosphere can also become heated as the ideas are developed and tested. Keuning wrote part of 'Mr. Brightside' in his closet, and now as the band is constantly on the road, **the confined tour bus has become the arena where the second album is forming.**

Keuning explained, 'Every song is different. The credits on the album give you a general idea of who did what. But some songs – like "Believe Me Natalie", for instance – Ronnie wrote a lot of that. Brandon wrote most of the music. After that, it took like a month of just the four of us in the garage hashing it out. We tried so many different parts – I'm sure we all wrote different parts at one time or another that even the author doesn't even know were thrown away.'

On the other hand, 'Smile Like You Mean It' took Mark Keuning a total of 8 minutes to compose but it also has the anthemic 'instant classic' feel with the simple but memorable imagery of the lyrics and the big sound.

PRETTY AND PINK:
The Band's Eighties Influences

Brandon is known for his taste in the kind of pink blazers that were trendy in the 80s and his fascination with the music of that era. Every reviewer of **Hot Fuss** inevitably reel off a list of its derivative influences because the album constantly walks the fine line between the homage and imitation of former rock legends.

> The anglophile/music connoisseur that developed in Utah has reanimated the heroes of his youth in his song writing, making his band a part of the 'NEW NEW WAVE MOVEMENT'.

The most hyped rock bands of the past few years have been part of this movement. Bands such as the White Stripes, Franz Ferdinand, and The Strokes, all pay tribute to the new-wave era of the Eighties, when Duran Duran and New Order songs were chart-toppers. However, The Killers layered in a stadium rock glitz, derived more from 90s' bands like U2 and Oasis, and more than their fellow 80s-infatuated rivals have the musicianship to bring it off.

For example, 'Somebody Told Me', both in its arrangement and subject matter, sounds remarkably similar to the chorus of the old Blur song 'Girls and Boys' ('Girls who are boys/ Who like boys to be girls/ Who do boys like they're girls').

And not only that, the song describes the feeling of attraction to a person that is already attached, which is not exactly an original concept. 'The song is a cliché,' admits Brandon.

'But that's good because it makes it more memorable. AND THAT'S WHAT YOU WANT SONGS TO BE.'

Flowers knows what he is doing. The right clichés resonate sentiments that people hold dear; they strike chords with which the public identifies. The trick is, however, to avoid being mundane and so, throughout *Hot Fuss*, the homages to David Bowie, Duran Duran, Depeche Mode and U2, surface with enough dynamism to sound innovative to naïve listeners and, for the music-savvy ear, like an anthemic throw-back.

Jay-Z, president of Def Jam Recordings (Island's sister label at the Universal Music Group) is obviously thrilled with the best-selling new rock band of the past year and, predictably, makes a virtue of their retro-leanings. 'I think they take what's old and make it sound new again,' Jay-Z commented. 'Do you know what I mean? I don't want to sound like some weirdo fan. But that's what they're doing…

'My favourite part of their song is when they repeat, "It was only a kiss! It was only a kiss!"

'But that's everyone's favourite part, right?'

Keuning identifies The Killers with the new-wave craze, proud of their role within it. 'There are some good music phases and I think we're fortunate to be part of one. Just think, in ten years, grunge will be back around and everyone will think that's the best music,' muses Keuning. 'When heavy metal died, all of this great music was given a chance to come to light.

'Music that people thought never had a chance was being listened to widely. Think about what Nirvana did for music. That's what this group of bands we're part of is like – Interpol, the Yeah Yeah Yeahs – so much great new music is coming out. We're honoured to be a part of this movement.'

However, despite the acclaim such bands have received from the critics, there are more than a few cynics who've called out for creativity not recycling.

The Killers have always been dogged by attempts to identify the influences for particular songs and speculation has been rife as to the exact allusions. Is a particular chorus reminiscent of Duran Duran or U2? Is Brandon's stage persona Ziggy Stardust take two?

But saying that the band is 'not real', that it's 'derivative', is missing the point. TS Eliot put it inimitably: **'While immature poets imitate, mature poets steal.'** Plundering the past is an art in itself, nonetheless the acid test is what is made of the plunder.

Inevitably it has fallen to Brandon to mount a defence to this charge of plagiarism and the controversy over the band's 'influences'. He said, 'Yeah, I don't understand it… Umm, it's really weird because… there's nothing that we've ripped off directly, you know what I mean?

'It's just us writing songs, not thinking about anything other than trying to write a good song.'

But constantly being accused of of lifting the work of past bands does get under the skin of The Killers. When asked about the Duran Duran and Depeche Mode comparisons, Brandon replied, 'It's not a totally bad thing. I love them. The only thing that's irritating about it is sometimes they're the only bands. We listen to so much other music. We are influenced by a lot of music... It's nice because we're trying to be timeless in a way. We hope to stand the test of time. Hopefully this album will be good five years from now.'

Stoermer is less reserved than Brandon in dismissing the charge as irrelevant: 'We aren't reinventing the wheel. We are just taking inspiration from bands we like and making a new sound.'

Critical analysis can, as we see in film, become so caught up with analysing its own interpretations that it becomes a solipsistic enterprise. Serious criticism of rock music is showing a similar tendency.

Liam Gallagher put it rather more succinctly: 'They're not listening to our music, they're sniffing their own arses.'

Whatever the artistic conclusion of 'the test of time', the commercial one is already in. The creative, seductive larceny of The Killers has paid off. **Hot Fuss** has spawned two top ten hits on Billboard's Modern Rock Tracks with 'Mr. Brightside' and 'Somebody Told Me'. By summer 2005, the album had sold over 2 million copies and remains steadily in the Billboard top 200.

Moreover, The Killers have not merely sold records - 2004 was a year of accolades and recognition from the award committees.

They won the ESKY award for 'Best Rookies' from Esquire magazine, were the band nominated for two Brit Awards, three Meteors, and the Shortlist Prize.

Even the Record Academy could not resist bestowing three GRAMMY nominations on the blast-from-the-past sound of The Killers. 'Somebody Told Me' received two nominations, Best Rock Song and Best Rock Performance by a duo or group with vocal, while **Hot Fuss** itself earned a nomination for Best Rock Album.

Hitting the Road
THE KILLERS ON TOUR

With the release of their debut album, The Killers embarked on a non-stop concert tour, constantly jet-lagging between the States, Europe, Japan, and Australia. As their fame snowballed, they performed in larger and larger venues, from intimate bars with a hundred fans to music festivals with their thousands. And this marathon touring schedule did not stop for at least a year and a half, until they headed back to Vegas and the recording studio in October 2005.

Hot Fuss hints at the flashy edge of the band's style, but only seeing them strut their stuff live conveys their true flamboyance and edginess. 'I think we are a whole different thing live than on record,' Stoermer has asserted. 'We bring a whole load of energy and we definitely try to make every performance something special...

'We're more raw, more brutal on stage. When we connect with the audience and they connect with us, amazing things happen.'

Soon after the album's release, the band arrived in New York to play the Bowery Ball Room on 16 August 2004. The gigs were booked out but the audience was not fawning at their feet until after they'd finished their opening number, 'Jenny was a Friend of Mine'. Straight over to his synth rack, Brandon's toe-tapping tinkling was joined with the exploding guitar riffs echoing from the cloud of frizz that is Dave Keuning. As the band went through 'Change Your Mind', 'Midnight Show', 'Indie Rock 'n' Roll' and 'Mr. Brightside', the crowd became more and more feverish. Vannucci's thumping escalated to seizure-like zeal, fists filled the air and the sing-along voices louder.

One of the most amusing elements of a Killers' concert is to see the audience belting out the rather disturbing lyrics of murder and jealousy with carefree joy. As MTV.com memorably phrased it, the New York concert was no different:

'There was something odd and beautiful about hundreds of people bouncing on the ballroom's floor and singing along "It's all in my head/ But she's touching his chest now/ He takes off her dress now/ Let me go", all of them seemingly sharing in the paranoid fantasy, or at least indulging Flowers' fixation.'

On this summer night in NYC, the trend-setting crowd was clearly out-done by Brandon's perfectly gelled hair, snappy, cream-coloured jacket and blue collared shirt. Glistening with glitter and the sheen of sweat, Brandon finished the set with the crowd-pleaser 'Somebody Told Me' and finally the up-and-coming hit 'All These Things I've Done'. And his formula of over-indulgent rock-out sorrow combined with knock-'em-dead style was a success once again; a deafening roar greeted the performance.

The only hiccup was towards the end of the set, when Brandon ripped his hand on one of Ronnie's cymbals. It bled profusely. He hid it from the audience, then one of the crew staunched the wound with gaffer tape. Brandon didn't use it to hustle any sympathy, but it was announced when they went off that, because of the injury, there'd be a delay before they came out for the encore .

'Like so many of the bands that influenced them – New Order, the Psychedelic Furs and even Oasis to a degree – The Killers are about feeling terrible and looking fabulous,' MTV.com has said. And the band's hot style has become one their premier calling cards, attracting almost as much attention as their music.

The mix of superficial style and genuine substance, a throwback to the new-wave days, is part of a consciously crafted image. 'I didn't come out of the womb like this,' Flowers said, gesturing at himself. 'When we signed with Island, we said, "We want to be successful." But we still want credibility. You don't want to lose the kids.' The cynic might add, 'Especially as they buy the records.' Brandon is claiming, however, a cred based on the experience The Killers deliver. And just as they don't rip off other artists, they don't rip off their fans with faux product. Like the band is more than the parts, their act is a lot more than their music.

Whether their music will stand the test of time is one thing, but The Killers are not phoneys. THEY'RE FOR REAL.

The Killers learned the hard way that image is everything in the music industry: 'Every label said no,' recalled Flowers caustically. Their rejection by Warner Music and other American labels back in 2002 still rankles.

'They said I didn't have SEX APPEAL or CHARISMA on stage.

'That's when I realised how much the whole package has to do with it.

'I went out and bought a bunch of concert movies: *Ziggy Stardust*, *Rattle and Hum*, *Gimme Shelter*.

I'd like to say you just go up there and play your songs. Some people can do that. But there's also something special about going over the top.'

And flashy clothes are only part of the package; The Killers are always looking to up the ante on their performance. They have a rich theatrical heritage to mine, as well. 'We come from Vegas so we've developed some showmanship,' Keuning said. 'With this kind of music, there's a certain level of flamboyance that's expected and we hope we can deliver. Image has always been an important part of rock and roll. It should never overshadow the music, but it should complement it. When we were practicing in a 128-Fahrenheit garage, we weren't wearing Prada suits, but it wouldn't seem right for us to come out playing our music in jeans and T-shirts and a trucker cap.'

As suit after dapper suit appeared on stage, Brandon has become something of a fashion icon. He takes some flak for his taste. His Chanel shades, which he dons no matter the lighting, *Rolling Stone* described as 'a designer version of the sunglasses old men in Florida wear after cataract surgery.' His similarly thick Gucci's are rumoured to be the women's version. Overall, though, the response is complimentary.

His adorable pink jacket appeared for the first time on an NME Awards tour and got rave reviews.

Acknowledging his fashionista status, Flowers has taken his retro suit style to another level: 'I'm on a mission to bring back the boat shoe,' he recently claimed. In July 2005, he even made the pages of the *Sunday Times Style* Magazine.

Brandon's peacock wardrobe makes headlines in fashion publications **and teenage girlies at the gigs wet their knickers.**

On the other hand, it probably does not do much for the headbangers in the mosh pit.

The band ended their North American tour with a spectacular at the Las Vegas House of Blues, on September 19th. They returned home to a rapturous welcome that celebrated them for what they'd become – rock 'n' roll stars. The House of Blues was heaving with a sell-out 1,800. When they were waiting to come on set, the lights dimmed and the curtain rose, then to rev up the crowd the sound system blasted out Frankie Vallie's 'You're Just Too Good To Be True.'

Brandon strode out, snapped the mike from the stand and said, 'Hello, we're called The Killers.' The audience erupted.

As soon as the band started to open with 'Jenny Was a Friend of Mine', the expectant crowd turned into a massive tumult of dancing bodies. Everyone on the floor was singing and swaying along with the beat – this was rocking with the music and celebrating the hometown band that had rocked the world.

After burning through 'On Top', Flowers introduced 'Mr Brightside' by saying, 'This next song has been around a while. You might've heard it at Tramps or something.' Next to 'Somebody Told Me': Brandon intro'd it with the words: 'The next one is for all of you that doubted.'

The band ended on 'All These Things I've Done'. The ecstatic crowd drowned out the band on the climactic chorus, chanting 'I've got soul, but I'm not a soldier.' Before leaving the stage, the four stood before the crowd visibly affected emotionally, honouring the reception they had received. Brandon said, 'You've all made us feel at home, which is how we should feel.'

After this triumphant gig, The Killers made their way back to Europe to an even more ecstatic response from the audience.

'I FEEL OVERWHELMED,' Flowers said to cheers in London. 'Every time we come back to England, you guys are so amazing, and your reactions have filtered back to America. You figured it out before they did.'

Brandon had always raved about England. On their second visit, he'd said: 'It's great. I mean, we're all lovers of English rock. To go there and have our first gig there was something that will stand out forever. NME was there, and that was such a big deal to us. And we're playing in places where Blur and Oasis started playing. We were just so excited.'

But their meteoric rise drew some flak from rivals about their retro-style. When the Canadian band The Stills and the New York group Secret Machines accused The Killers of not being 'real', Flowers rebutted it in the London listings magazine *Time Out*: 'Both those bands have an American attitude where it's not cool to be popular.'

Vannucci added, 'When you meet a new band in the UK and you're sharing a bill they say, "Hey, you're a musician too? Nice to meet you." It's different in the US. They say, "Oh, you're in The Killers? **Are you a fag? Are you wearing eye-liner?**" You just get static in the States.'

The Killers have felt more welcome and more at home in the UK, where their musical roots lie. This was never better illustrated than at the Kentish Town Forum in August 2002, when they were playing 'Andy, You're a Star'. A teenage girl threw her panties at Brandon who picked them up, twirled them on his finger, then without clocking the mobile number felt-tipped onto the crotch, cavalierly tossed them aside. This was as confident as Brandon gets. Even in June 2005, he admitted that his demons still get to him on stage. After that particular show, he said, 'I still don't banter much when I'm up there. I never know what to say.'

He doesn't need to, THE MUSIC DOES THE DANCING.

Of course, their image is all very non-PC for rock 'n' roll. Bands are supposed give the groupies some bragging rights, host way-out parties and put the the local drug dealers on the payroll. However, The Killers, two of whom are now married, the other two with serious girlfriends, don't do the classic rock star number, instead, whether on or off the road, they make a virtue of their rather dorky, calm lifestyle.

Stoermer corrected one reporter fishing for some racy copy: 'We are pretty quiet guys. It's funny you tell someone you're in a band and they immediately think you've done something wrong. . . We try to avoid doing that.'

After all, geeky is the new cool or, at least, The Killers hope so.

Brandon Flowers is a Mormon, which fascinates the press. Not since Donny Osmond has there been a singer with such sexual appeal who is also a card-carrying member of the Church of Latter Day Saints or Mormon Church. And on an interesting side note, Brandon shares more with Donny than religious preference and career choice, he also has similar theatrical aspirations. Donny Osmond performed in **Phantom of the Opera** for years, and Flowers has admitted his own interest in the musical: 'I saw **Phantom of the Opera** last time we were here,' he has said in 2005. 'So good. Andrew Lloyd Webber could have written rock hits.' Then, he exclaimed, 'I want to be the Phantom! Maybe when I'm, like, thirty. I can't do it now. I'd need to take voice lessons.' Did Donny?!

Incidentally, Donny like Brandon also ducked serving his 'mission' and seemingly shares some of Brandon's lack of confidence as, at one stage, he had to seek treatment for Social Anxiety Disorder. Perhaps singing Mormons who shirk their religious duties become vulnerable to stage fright.

At first, Brandon tried to keep stum about his rather unusual religious devotion, claiming the band did not want him to discuss it. However, as reporters kept coming back to it, he went out of his way to elaborate his position, desperately trying not to sound too Cliff Richard-y.

Flowers explained, 'Being a Mormon is just like following any religion. It's not much different than a lot of them. But it's difficult sometimes when you are on the road...

'We are faced with a lot of things on a daily basis that most people don't face, like SEX, DRUGS AND ROCK 'N' ROLL. How you handle that depends on what type of person you are.

'I guess we're pretty boring, but there is occasional drinking and smoking. I think compared to most bands we're well behaved. It's fine for some and you get away with these things in moderation... But most of us have had girlfriends the whole time we've been in the group so groupies have always been kept at bay.'

Although more open about his faith now, Brandon still gets touchy. *Rolling Stone* captured one awkward encounter with a fan who made a joke about his Mormonism.

'Hey, Brandon,' the kid asked, 'how many wives do you have?' 'That's funny,' Flowers answered dryly, not looking at the kid at all, 'except polygamy ended about a hundred and fifty years ago.'

Actually it didn't, but it put the kid in his place. In general, he tends to downplay his faith, trying to come over as cool, not squeaky-clean. He is always keen to point out that he still drinks and smokes... moderately. Yet he can become irate at any suggestion that not doing the prescribed excesses limits The Killers' music.

'It bothers me that I'd be more credible to certain people if I had a drug problem. Why? That's bullshit. I'm not interested in drugs because I've seen what they can do. Take Brian Wilson. I don't want to be like him. What does it matter today that he wrote "Good Vibrations"? The man goes round talking about himself to himself. Drugs fuck people up. None of us are into being fucked up.'

So for anyone who's interested, Brandon doesn't only drink and smoke, moderately, he also swears, moderately. Thus, he is in flagrant breach of the 'Word of Wisdom', the Mormon dietary code that calls for abstinence from alcohol, tobacco, coffee, tea, and profanities.

Brandon, then, is pretty wild...
FOR A MORMON.

He is the only Mormon in the group, but the other three are not dissimilar in their views. Vannucci makes the point that they are not small-town boys suddenly let loose in the candy store:

'We get offered drugs all the time, but we come from Vegas, man... We've seen it all. That shit doesn't surprise us. I think it's pretty rock 'n' roll not to do drugs, right?'

Moving in the circles of the modern rock pantheon, the band came into contact with many of their idols. As touring continued in 2005, the band met most of their major influences on their list: 'In the last couple of weeks, we've met Noel, Elton John, Bono and Morrissey. Getting recognised by these people is one of the most important things for me. If they didn't like us it would be a disaster,' Brandon admitted.

Meeting Bono was particularly significant to Brandon, as he wants The Killers to emulate U2: 'U2 are a great example of a band that has integrity, staying power and the songs. Their songs are so good and so big, the band no longer owns them. Those songs are now public property.'

Bono has actually endorsed the band. He bestowed a memorable compliment on The Killers, making the band's day:

'It's rare to find a band that not only have the music but a lyricist too. I HEAR THE KILLERS AND I GET OFF THE PHONE.'

Even fans of The Killers can miss how ambitious they are. They are not satisfied with the meteoric breakthrough to stardom, they want to enter that inner sanctuary of stadium rock tourers who, like Elton, U2, the Stones, Madonna, Oasis, keep the show on the road, year after year after year.

Despite the buzz of touring and meeting the members of their new club, Flowers knows that the band is becoming jaded: 'We're still just playing gigs every day. The only thing different is maybe the hotels are a little nicer.' Nagging at the back of his mind, too, is the way performing and touring restricts the time available to practice and create. He more than the others is only too aware that if the band is to realise its ambitions it must develop, innovate, evolve…

For the past year and a half, the band has hardly been able to take a breather, but Brandon did take some time out, in Hawaii, to get married to Tana Munbkowsky on 2 August 2005 with the other three band-members as witnesses. Tana, 23 years old, studied IT at the Community College of Southern Nevada, then went on to become a manageress of Urban Outfitters, which is located in the Mandalay Palace.

Urban Outfitters is an American chain that specialises in casual clothing. She also modelled some of their items in a feature in the *Las Vegas CityLife* weekly newspaper. She converted to Mormonism after she met Brandon but, by all accounts, that did not figure in his intention to marry her. 'I would have married her regardless,' he emphasised to one Vegas newspaper.

'There were no ultimatums, but while I was away she got involved in it.' They are setting up house on the outskirts of Vegas in a city called Henderson, which attracted Brandon as it has numerous golf courses.

Their last tour date scheduled is in October, and with Brandon's wistful descriptions of his home, the desire to take a break from touring is obvious: 'Lately, I've become very sentimental about my home. THE DESERT IS SO PRETTY AND LAS VEGAS IS THIS BEAUTIFUL, COLOURFUL CITY IN THE MIDDLE OF IT. I love going to casinos, shopping and eating.'

A KILLER of a name

Of course, there is an informal meaning of kill, which is to overwhelm someone with emotion. At the same time, The Killers resonates with the origins of the Strip and the murder of founding mobsters like Bugsy Seigal. It also associates neatly with the only other Vegas group to break out of the locale, Slaughter. As a name for this glitzy band from Vegas, The Killers is definitely a copywriter's hit.

Curiously enough, their eventual manager, Brandon Merrick, picked up on them because of the lethal overtones of the group's name. He'd been repping for Warner Bros. and was just checking out local bands on LVlocalmusicscene.com., when he saw their listing. The name intrigued him, so contacted them and listened to a demo tape of 'Somebody Told Me'.

As an insider put, Merrick felt 'the money shot'. This is the 'instant classic' feel that record executives are always searching for: it's that part of a song that when you hear it hits you right in the solar plexus and knocks you out. It gets you where it counts – in your feelings and, next, your pocket. You want to listen to the record, watch the gig, buy the album and go with the feeling. The money shot is the music that the record industry wants to hear.

Merrick wanted to sign the band up with Warner Bros. but they turned them down before he secured a deal with Lizard King. According to him his '… arrangement with Warner Bros. was that I was a consultant, which allowed me to have a management company. I've also produced some acts, as well. But when I saw The Killers, it was just like, "This is what I'm gonna do." I was doing some development stuff, really looking for that act.

'I'd done some training with Grateful Dead's management, worked with Billy Joel's manager, stuff like that. I always wanted to break out on my own, so I really did it in forging a career as a manager with this band.

'I'm very grateful and happy about that.'

So are the press boys. A popular band with a name like The Killers is a godsend for reporters as they can wordplay with the headlines to their hearts content. The following are typical of the catchy one-liners and cheesy puns that they have generated:

ARE YOU DYING TO SEE THIS SHOW?: MICROSCOPE ON THE KILLERS

LIVE: THE KILLERS MURDER AT THE MOD

KILLERS TO KEEP RACKING UP THE BODY COUNT THROUGH NOVEMBER

THE LADY KILLER: AN INTERVIEW WITH THE KILLERS' BRANDON FLOWERS

THE KILLERS SLAY CLUBLAND WITH REMIXES

THE KILLERS ARE KNOCKING 'EM DEAD, INCLUDING BONO, BOWIE AND ELTON

HIT MEN: FUELLED BY EYELINER AND A LOVE OF THE '80S, THE KILLERS ARE THE BIGGEST NEW BAND OF THE YEAR

CRIME SCENE INVESTIGATION: HOW DID BRANDON FLOWERS, RONNIE VANNUCCI, DAVE KEUNING AND MARK STOERMER GO FROM THE LAS VEGAS DIVE BAR CIRCUIT TO SELLING FOUR MILLION COPIES OF THEIR DEBUT ALBUM, *HOT FUSS*?

Moreover, killers by name, killers by music. They sing about murderers. And as a result, they have provoked some of the same criticism that gothic music and rap gets. Social pundits and politicians looking for fall guys to railroad for rising gun crime – especially school massacres – are always fingering rock music with violent lyrics. And, let's face it, the culprits do listen to it; but then so does everyone else. To put a spin on Frankie Vallie's hit: It's too bad to be true.

Nonetheless, The Killers have been put in the same dock as the rapping ex·crackheads with their pop·a·cap·in·yer·ass doggerel.

The most contentious of The Killers' songs, 'Where is She?', sparked a firestorm of protests, even before its official release. Scheduled to appear on their second album, the song recounts the death of a young girl, inspired by the actual murder of the fourteen-year-old Jodi Jones. Jodi's boyfriend, Luke Mitchell, was charged with the crime, and the court sentenced him to a minimum of 20 years in prison.

Ironically enough, music became the culprit during the highly publicised trial at Edinburgh's High Court. The prosecution stressed that Luke Mitchell had often listened to Marilyn Manson and went on to suggest that the murder scene appeared to mirror one of the goth singer's paintings, The Black Dahlia. It could not prove the connection between the singer and Luke's violent act, but the creepy possibility that the Jodi's death was a twisted homage to Manson remained in the air.

Brandon should have known that his own song drawn from these events would add fuel to the charge that such music inflames immature minds.

The media did call into question the band's choice of subject matter. One journalist bluntly spelled it out: 'Real-life tragedies are not a topic for modern pop songs.'

The *Sunday Herald* reported the concerns of a friend of the Jones family: 'The nightmare scenario is that someone close to Jodi would unexpectedly hear the song on the radio.'

The newspaper quoted the friend: 'Can you imagine hearing a song about your child who has been killed? It seems dreadful.'

Brandon first heard about the murder in January of 2004 during Luke's trial, while in Glasgow for the NME Awards Tour. Spurred to record the tragic events, he began to write a song, attempting to capture the real-life drama in lyrics and sound. He told MTV about his muse: 'This teenage kid asked his girlfriend to come to his house and he was waiting in the woods on the way to his house... It was dark and he just brought her in there and cut her up.'

In this nonchalant interview, Flowers claimed that the song would be written from the perspective of Jodi's mother, Judy, as if she was speaking to the murderer. The chorus echoes the poignant questions of a grief-stricken mother to the murderer: 'Where is she?/ Where is my baby girl?/ I've seen you/ And you're crazy/ What have you done with my whole wide world?'

Brandon did not get a good press on this one. As one reviewer put it: 'To condense a murder into three minutes of jiggy-ass pop music is asking for trouble. Especially if the name of your band is The Killers.'

The band's mobiles – especially Brandon's – were doing their own jangling jig as the 'money shot' execs bombarded the four with damage-limitation scripts.

Brandon back-pedalled, apologised and down-played. He told the press: 'There's no way on earth I could ever possibly pretend to know what it must actually feel like to suffer such a thing, and I wouldn't presume to appropriate any other individual's feelings for a song. Rather, seeing those news stories got me to thinking about the powerlessness and frustration that must come from losing a child like that, and it was from those thoughts that "Where Is She?" came to be.'

But no songwriter or money shot exec is going to kill a good song to suck up to the spokespersons of the moral/silent majority. 'Where Is She?' will be on the next album.

The name of the band, though, will continue to generate publicity, which good or bad will generally push up sales. Yet, despite it being a publicist's dream, the origins of the band's name lie in the mundane and contingent. Ronnie Vannucci acknowledged the media buzz that surrounded the name even back in 2002 and explained that they chose 'The Killers' simply because...

'IT SOUNDED COOL.'

'I think there are far more offensive names out there like Nashville Pussy, Cryptic Slaughter and Julio Iglesias. **Personally, I think Julio Iglesias is far more offensive than the aforementioned names.'**

In fact, Brandon and Keuning had been watching a New Order music video called 'Crystal, which depicted a fictional band. Printed inconspicuously on the bass drum was 'The Killers'. As the fake band was a perfect group with the prescribed accoutrements of youth, good looks, talent and fuck-me groupies, they decided instantly and unanimously that 'The Killers' it was.

Of course, as they were already writing songs with more than a touch of the Sweeney Todds, the name fitted.

One of The Killers' trademarks is songs with sinister themes eerily submerged in a cheerful beat and jubilant guitar riffs. At a Killers' concert, lyrics about paranoia, obsession, murder, rage, and despair, put to an appealing beat, float melodically from the stage. Two songs on the album, 'Jenny was a Friend of Mine' and 'Midnight Show', in combination with the unreleased 'Leave the Bourbon on the Shelf', form a single storyline, which The Killers have dubbed 'The Murder Trilogy'.

In the three songs, Flowers wails out the tale of a jealous boyfriend who murders his wayward girlfriend and then gets caught by the police. Embracing the sensationalistic and the dark, the band plans to film a 25-minute movie based around the murder story with the three songs as a soundtrack. It is black humour, rock–style.

'The crashing tide can't hide a
guilty girl
With jealous hearts that start
with gloss and curls
I took my baby's breath beneath
the chandelier
Of stars in atmosphere
And watch her disappear
Into the midnight show...'

Stephen Sondheim eat your heart out... Well, not quite.

Hoping to finish the project by the end of 2005, the band has met with various Hollywood directors and actors in an effort to fill the gap between *Hot Fuss* and their second album. 'We talk about it every day; it's just a matter of timing,' bassist Mark Stoermer said. 'It's cutting it close now because we'd like to do it before the next album comes out.'

The Killers plan to take the film to the Sundance Film Festival, and rumours on the Internet suggest that they plan on distributing the film on DVD in some kind of giveaway to a selection of lucky fans.

Summing up the scope of this ambitious project, drummer Vannucci told Billboard.com: 'IT'S KIND OF LIKE OUR *THRILLER*.'

This was slightly before rock music's licensed paedophile just escaped the slammer by the skin of his whitened, much re-shaped nose. Rest assured The Killers will not be making anymore comparisons with *Thriller*.

Rock Rivalry
SUCCESS CAN SUCK

The Killers' extraordinary success has had its price. The inevitable clingers-on, grasping for a piece of the pie, have given the band grief, and Brandon has not been shy in ranting to the press about what's crawled out of the woodwork.

For example, the former drummer, Buss Bradley, who seemed to disappear without a trace in the early days of the band, returned with a vengeance. He attempted to sue The Killers, claiming that he had written 'Mr. Brightside'.

A resigned Brandon commented: 'This guy who was in my band a long time ago is trying to sue us. We wrote "Mr. Brightside" a long, long time ago, when we had a different drummer. He had nothing to do with it, but his wife is a lawyer, so she just sent a letter to our lawyer. You always hear about people coming out of the woodwork once you get big, but this is... wow.'

Although the lawsuit eventually disappeared, Flowers remained particularly sensitive to the threat of others capitalising on the band's success. And perhaps spurred by this anxiety, Brandon suddenly began to bang on to the press about another band that has to some extent pirated The Killers or, as some might say, copycatted what The Killers had pirated.

The Bravery, a band from New York City, was creating a modest stir, especially in the UK. But in comparison with The Killers, The Bravery remained on the fringe of the industry. However, Brandon, in a March 2005 interview with MTV.com, raised his freshly polished boat shoe to squash this rather insignificant bug. Questioning The Bravery's authenticity and originality, Flowers incited a feud that has continued to rage throughout the year and in doing so put Bravery on a much bigger map than they had been hitherto .

The super-stylish Bravery have the same publicist, are on the same record label, and have similar creative influences, lifting from the 80s' Brit pop rock cannon in a manner very much like The Killers. All of this hit just a little too close to home for Brandon.

Sounding like he was back
on the coffee and tea again, he took
the hammer to the nutshell: 'I've heard rumours
about a member of that band being in a different
kind of band. How do you defend that? If you say, "My
heart really belongs to what I'm doing now," but you used to
be in a ska band. I can see The Strokes play or Franz Ferdinand
play and it's real, and I haven't gotten that from The Bravery."

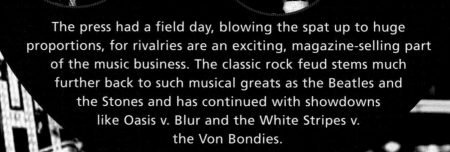

The press had a field day, blowing the spat up to huge
proportions, for rivalries are an exciting, magazine-selling part
of the music business. The classic rock feud stems much
further back to such musical greats as the Beatles and
the Stones and has continued with showdowns
like Oasis v. Blur and the White Stripes v.
the Von Bondies.

Caught up in the excitement, the BBC even went so far as to wittily define rock rivalry: 'The classic rock feud requires two bands of direct opposites. They should hail from different geographical locations, preferably different classes, and ideally should be convinced they operate at different ends of the musical spectrum, while actually making music that is distinctly similar to their rivals. And if you can chuck in an element of brain versus brawn, then so much the better.'

Oasis are rock 'n' roll's Mike Tyson. They are always looking to bite a rival's ear. After Blur faded from the scene, they turned on Coldplay, whom the Gallaghers dubbed a bunch of 'bed-wetters'. Liam, naturally, expressed his appreciation of The Killers and The Bravery trading insults.

He told The Bravery, 'It's really good to see bands fighting again.'

Given their starburst into the galaxy of rock, it was predictable that The Killers would be asked by Bob Geldof to appear at his Live 8 concert in Hyde Park on 2 June 2005. They featured with such luminaries as the veteran anti-poverty campaigner Madonna ('Are you fucking ready London?') and Kofi Annan who thankfully didn't sing, just spontaneously *ducted* some oil-for-food crocodile tears. Perhaps Brandon did his own bit to save the world by converting her and our UN Secretary-General to Mormonism. Those two on a 'mission trip', extended and together, might not do much for poverty in Africa but it would do wonders for morale everywhere else.

Decked out in white suits and looking like a Barber Shop quartet working an ocean liner, The Killers did only one number, 'All These Things That I've Done'. But it left everyone, including Robbie Williams, wishing for more. At least, Robbie tried to make amends by working into his set the refrain, 'I've got soul but I'm not a soldier'. Brandon said afterwards, 'I didn't know it was going to happen. I've never met him, but it was cool. Nice of him.'

The Killers' big challenge of 2005 is producing a humdinger of a new album. They finished touring in October, then they headed back to Las Vegas to go into studio. Dave Keuning commented,

'We all still call Vegas home, and that's where we want to settle for a little bit, and go to our own homes at night. We're still looking for a studio but we may end up building our own.'

The new album is already taking shape as they have some twenty or so new tracks – including the controversial 'Where Is She?' – to choose from. It is rumoured that 'Uncle Johnny Did Cocaine' has been cut (if that is the right term). 'All The Pretty Faces', a guitar-driven tale of love turned bad will almost certainly make it. One thing's for sure, it will be a *humkiller* of an album, that will eclipse the sales of **Hot Fuss,** delight the fans and keep the money shot execs singing along all the way to the bank.

'We always wanted the bigness,' admits Flowers. 'A lot of times people just don't have the ability to write songs like we do and they hide behind the idea that they are underground or indie. But if they could write a song like we can, I think they would in a second.'

The chorus line of 'Glamorous indie Rock & Roll' is 'It's indie rock 'n' roll for me/ It's all I need'. The Killers are using pop to roll indie-Rock into the mosh pit, which is exactly where it should be.

'We're not claiming to have any kind of fucking Holy Grail to rock 'n' roll,' says Vannucci. 'We're just a rock band that writes good pop songs.

'IS THAT SO HARD TO BELIEVE?'